POWELL V. SUPERPULPER, INC.

Second Edition

POWELL V. SUPERPULPER, INC.

Second Edition

Andrew J. Stern, Esq.

Kline & Specter, P.C.

Gwen Roseman Stern, Esq.

Director of Trial Advocacy and Professor of Law
Drexel University Thomas R. Kline School of Law

Samuel A. Haaz, Esq.

Philadelphia District Attorney's Office

NITA®
NATIONAL INSTITUTE FOR TRIAL ADVOCACY

Address inquiries to:

Reprint Permission
National Institute for Trial Advocacy
1685 38th Street, Suite 200
Boulder, CO 80301-2735
Phone: (800) 225-6482
Fax: (720) 890-7069
E-mail: permissions@nita.org

ISBN 978-1-60156-492-4 (print)
eISBN 978-1-60156-532-7 (eBook)
FBA 1492

Printed in the United States of America

Acknowledgments

Thanks to Andrew Bond, for his tireless assistance in helping to create this second edition of this case file. Thanks also to Professor Gwen Stern's former law students, Elia Robertson and Peter Johnson, for their research and contributions.

We also acknowledge Michelle Windsor, our NITA editor, for her excellent editing comments and guidance.

CONTENTS

Exhibits

A Note from the Authors

This brief note provides some background information and additional instruction on how to best utilize this unique NITA case file. Although the names and witnesses have been changed, the depicted events are based on an actual case that was litigated and tried by Andrew J. Stern as lead counsel. Indeed, some of the photographs and animations are identical to those materials used as trial exhibits in the initial case. This detailed fact pattern and supporting illustrative exhibits will provide law students and trial lawyers with an opportunity to creatively and effectively argue their respective theories. *Powell v. SuperPulper, Inc.* can be applied to teach trial advocacy techniques on both liability and/or damages. In that regard, the liability and damage phase contains its own witnesses and exhibits to facilitate bifurcation or to allow trial as one matter. In sum, our goal was to create a case file that teaches realistic trial advocacy techniques to students, but would also challenge trial lawyers who seek the thrill of perfecting their craft by trying this fascinating case.

We suggest that the reader view the animation of the hydrapulper before reading the file to see what a hydrapulper looks like and how it operates. It may also be helpful to review the jury instruction as a good starting point to the learn product liability law in the state of Nita.

Depending on which party you are assigned to represent, you will be acting as co-lead counsel with either:

Andrew J. Roseman, Esquire-Attorney for the Plaintiff

Gwen R. Sheppard, Esquire-Attorney for the Defense

Their names appear on the documents for each respective side.

Have fun!

Electronic versions of the exhibits are available for download here http://bit.ly/1P20Jea

Password: Powell2

INTRODUCTION

On January 9, 2015, Robin Powell filed a wrongful death and survival suit against SuperPulper, Inc. ("SuperPulper"). The suit alleged that SuperPulper manufactured a product called a hydrapulper that was allegedly defective due to a lack of sufficient guarding and warnings on and around the hydrapulper. Robin Powell's husband, Steven Powell, died while working one of SuperPulper's hydrapulper machines at a paper plant called Giant Paper, Inc. ("Giant Paper") in Nita City. Steve was an employee at Giant Paper.

On July 9, 2013, Steven Powell fell into a hydrapulper at Giant Paper. Although Mr. Powell had worked at Giant Paper for approximately twelve years, he had only started working on the hydrapulper a few days before the accident. Giant Paper is one of the leading manufacturers of corrugated cardboard and uses recycled paper to produce finished cardboard and other paper products. Giant Paper is not a party to this case. Although they employed Mr. Powell, the plaintiffs are not suing Giant Paper because this is a product liability case. The product Mr. Powell was using at the time of the accident was the hydrapulper that was designed, produced, and installed by the manufacturer, SuperPulper. SuperPulper installed the floor-fed hydrapulper at the Giant Paper plant in 2001.

A floor-fed hydrapulper is the first large piece of equipment used in the process of making commercial paper and cardboard boxes. The hydrapulper is like an oversized mixing bowl that chops up recycled paper products in very hot water (170 degrees Fahrenheit), creating a hot paper stock that has the consistency of thick mud. This stock is created from recycled paper and cardboard, which is ordinarily fed into the hydrapulper by a forklift. The forklift is used to push large bales of the recycled product into a hole in the floor. The mouth of the hydrapulper, where the paper is fed through a feed hole, is located at floor level. A steel cable was located in front of the feed hole that was supposed to serve as a sufficient guard and warning to keep workers away from the feed hole and to prevent accidental entry into the hydrapulper. On the day of the accident, Mr. Powell's designated forklift was broken and was being repaired nearby. Thus, he did not have a forklift available to help him push the bales of paper into the hydrapulper. There were no witnesses to the accident, but it was believed that Mr. Powell was cleaning loose paper scraps near the mouth of the hydrapulper and that he must have "gotten too close" and slipped and fell into the hydrapulper.

The day of the accident, a coworker heard Mr. Powell screaming, ran toward the hydrapulper, and saw Mr. Powell stuck in the thick, hot, paper pulp. His coworkers also saw that Mr. Powell was moving in a slow circular fashion and that he was being pulled down to the bottom where the auger chops up the stock. No retrieval equipment was readily available, so workers attempted to grab his hands and arms, but Mr. Powell's skin sloughed off as they grabbed at him. Ultimately, one of the workers was able to pull him out by his belt buckle. Mr. Powell was fully conscious when he was removed, and he was screaming, "I'm hot! I feel like I'm on fire!" It was evident that most of Mr. Powell's skin had been stripped away and his body was still steaming. No one knows for sure how long Mr. Powell was in the vat before he was discovered. Mr. Powell was emergently transported by ambulance to a local Nita hospital. He died the day after the accident.

Required Stipulations

1. The parties agree that the defendant, SuperPulper, has a nondelegable duty to include all elements of safety of the product and therefore there are no claims of action against the decedent's employer, Giant Paper, or any other entity.

2. The parties agree that the hydrapulper in question did not have any maintenance issues and was in good working order at the time of the decedent's accident.

3. There is no "state of the art" defense, and the defendant cannot introduce what types of guards are being used by other hydrapulper manufacturers.

4. The parties stipulate that in the damages portion of this trial, damages for 1) the defendant's liability and 2) for the plaintiff's pain and suffering are the only monetary damages the plaintiff seeks. Damages for the plaintiff's lost wages, or for any other reason aside from the two reasons mentioned, are not at issue in this case.

5. The parties stipulate that the decedent would have had a normal life expectancy.

6. All exhibits have been authenticated to be admissible at trial, but any other evidentiary objections are still permitted.

7. The parties stipulate that an emergency stop device on the hydrapulper would not have prevented the decedent's injuries.

8. The parties agree that the decedent did not have a heart attack or any medical condition that caused him to fall into the hydrapulper.

9. The parties agree that foul play did not cause the decedent to fall in the hydrapulper.

10. Giant Paper reasonably relied on SuperPulper to create the appropriate training and instructional video that Giant Paper would make available to its employees.

11. A normal pulse for a male of the decedent's height and weight is seventy beats per minute.

12. The pictures of the area around the hydrapulper were taken the day after the accident.

IN THE UNITED STATES DISTRICT COURT
FOR THE DISTRICT OF NITA

Robin Powell, Individually and as Administratrix of the Estate of Steven Powell, Decedent, Plaintiff v. SuperPulper, Inc. Defendant	:	CIVIL ACTION 9-2015 COMPLAINT

COMPLAINT

Now comes the plaintiff, Robin Powell, individually and as Administratrix of the Estate of Steven Powell, deceased, states and alleges as follows:

Parties:

1. At all relevant times hereto, the plaintiff was and is a resident of the State of Nita.
2. The defendant was and is a New Jersey corporation.
3. At all times relevant hereto, the defendant transacted substantial business activity in the State of Nita by designing, manufacturing, selling, and installing hydrapulpers and other industrial equipment directly and/or indirectly into the stream of commerce by contracting with Giant Paper, Inc., and other paper mills in the State of Nita and in the county.
4. At all times relevant hereto, plaintiffs Robin Powell and the decedent, Steven Powell, were husband and wife and are residents and citizens of the State of Nita.
5. The parties are diverse citizens, and jurisdiction and venue are appropriate in the United States District Court for the District of Nita.

COUNT I

6. Plaintiff incorporates by reference paragraphs 1 through 5 inclusive, as though set forth at length herein.
7. On or about July 9, 2013, plaintiff's decedent was thirty-four years old and was an employee of Giant Paper, Inc.
8. While performing his duties as a hydrapulper operator at the Giant Paper plant, the plaintiff's decedent slipped and fell into an improperly guarded and defectively designed hydrapulper, causing severe burns and, ultimately, his death.
9. The subject hydrapulper was defectively designed, manufactured, distributed, sold, and/or installed by the defendant for reasons that include, inter alia, the following:

a. Failing to properly design, manufacture, and install said hydrapulper with a safe guard surrounding the feed hole of the hydrapulper;

b. Failing to properly test each hydrapulper relating to the potential for unreasonably dangerous slippery conditions surrounding the hydrapulper;

c. Failing to provide adequate and conspicuous warnings relating to the inherent dangers of said hydrapulper, including the need to stay clear of the feed hole;

d. Failing to protect users from accidentally slipping and falling into the feed hole during reasonably foreseeable and intended use of said product; and

e. Failing to provide a safety manual and other written instructions with clear, plain, and conspicuous language to protect foreseeable inexperienced users from inherent dangers of said hydrapulper.

10. As a direct and proximate result of one or more of the defective and unreasonably dangerous conditions of said hydrapulper, plaintiff's decedent accidentally slipped and fell into the feed hole of a hydrapulper and sustained devastating injuries set forth herein.

11. As a direct and proximate result of the said hydrapulper's defect, plaintiff's decedent sustained severe disabling injuries, which included, inter alia, the following and directly caused plaintiff's decedent to suffer a painful and untimely death:

a. sloughing of skin during removal from the hydrapulper;

b. fatal burns covering 80 percent of plaintiff's decedent's body;

c. hospitalization for two days in the burn unit at Nita City Hospital;

d. medication for severe pain and suffering;

e. disfigurement;

f. loss of ability to engage in activities relating to the enjoyment of life;

g. past and future loss of earnings and earning capacity;

h. substantial medical expenses;

i. funeral expenses;

j. loss of substantial child support for plaintiff's decedent's children;

k. loss of tutelage for plaintiff; and

l. other damages as provided by Nita law.

WHEREFORE, the plaintiff is entitled to damages against defendant SuperPulper, Inc., in the amount of over $75,000.00, thereby allowing plaintiff to avoid compulsory arbitration and permitting a jury trial in accordance with the local Nita rules.

COUNT II

12. Plaintiff incorporates by reference paragraphs 1 through 11, inclusive, as though set forth at length herein.

13. Prior to his death, plaintiff's decedent, Steven Powell, consciously and knowingly suffered the awareness of his impending, imminent death and suffered severe conscious pain and suffering and other debilitating injuries.

WHEREFORE, the plaintiff is entitled to damages against defendant SuperPulper, Inc., in the amount of over $75,000.00.

Date: January 9, 2015

Andrew J. Roseman

Andrew J. Roseman, Esquire
Attorney for Plaintiff
1 Market Street
Nita City, Nita 19102

IN THE UNITED STATES DISTRICT COURT
FOR THE DISTRICT OF NITA

Robin Powell, Individually and as Administratrix of the Estate of Steven Powell, Decedent, Plaintiff v. SuperPulper, Inc. Defendant	: : : : : : : : :	 CIVIL ACTION 9-2015 ANSWER

ANSWER

Now comes the defendant, SuperPulper, Inc., and answers the Complaint as follows:

1. Admitted.
2. Admitted.
3. Admitted.
4. Admitted.
5. Admitted.
6. Answering defendant incorporates by reference paragraphs 1 through 5 inclusive, as though set forth at length herein.
7. Admitted.
8. After reasonable investigation, answering defendant is without sufficient knowledge to answer paragraph 7.
9. Denied.
10. Denied.
11. Denied.
12. Defendant incorporates by reference paragraphs 1 through 11, inclusive, as though set forth at length herein.
13. Denied.

WHEREFORE, the defendant demands that judgment be entered in favor of the defendant, including an award of costs relating to the defense of this action.

FIRST AFFIRMATIVE DEFENSE

Any injuries sustained or suffered by Steven Powell at the time and place mentioned in the Complaint were caused, in whole or in part, by the assumption of the risk by Steven Powell.

WHEREFORE, the defendant demands that judgment be entered in favor of the defendant with the costs and disbursements of this action.

Date: February 3, 2015

Gwen R. Sheppard

Gwen R. Sheppard
Attorney for Defendant
201 West 44th Street
New York, NY 10036

Deposition of Robin Powell

My name is Robin Powell, and I live at 3400 Market Street in Nita City, Nita. I am thirty-two years old and was married to Steve Powell for ten years before he died. We have two children, Stevie and Sarah. Stevie is eight years old, and Sarah is six years old. I graduated from Upper Dublin High School in Nita City and that is the extent of my education. However, I am a teacher's aide at St. Catherine's elementary school. I was working twenty hours a week before Steve died, but now I have to work forty hours a week to try and support my family. It is very difficult to pay the bills because we relied on Steve's salary. Steve was thirty-four years old when he died.

Steve was such a happy-go-lucky kind of a guy. He always had a smile on his face. He had several friends at work, but especially liked Lowell Smith. He worked with him prior to working at Giant Paper. I can't remember what job they did together. I know that at Giant Paper, they would have lunch together. In fact, we had gone out a few times with Lowell and his wife.

Prior to his death, Steve and I would do all kinds of things together. We liked to hike, bike, and sometimes go to the shore in the summer. Things have all changed now because all I do is work and take care of the kids. Now that I am working full time, I had to hire a babysitter to take care of the kids when I am working. She picks up the kids from the bus and then babysits until I get home. Steve used to spend a lot of time with Stevie and Sarah, and they were all very close. My husband and Stevie loved to play baseball and soccer together. They would let Sarah play with them, too, although she could not throw or hit the ball like Stevie could.

Steve also graduated from Upper Dublin High School. We met when he was a senior and I was a sophomore, but we did not get married until I was twenty-four and he was twenty-six. After high school, Steve started working at Sampson Paper Company, but that went out of business a few years after he started there. He then started working for Giant Paper and worked there for around twelve years before he passed. When we first got married we lived in a row house.

After we were married for eight years, we saved enough money to move into a single family house in Nita. However, now that Steve is not here anymore, I had to sell the house and move into an apartment because I cannot pay the mortgage or the utility bills.

Steve had been working as a rewinder for all his years at Giant Paper. A rewinder is responsible for making sure that the paper is put correctly on the spool before it goes to the finisher. He was supposed to be promoted to a finisher, but Giant Paper passed him over when he was absolutely the one who was supposed to get the job. They gave the job to some younger guy, who I understood was way less qualified. When Steve didn't get the promotion, it was hard on our family. Steve was a recovering alcoholic, and when he didn't get the job, he started drinking again. His willpower only lapsed for about a week, and then he sought help and re-enrolled in AA meetings. I was very proud of Steve for his strength in the face of addiction and for beating his alcoholism. He has been sober for the last three years straight, except for about a week when he was passed up for the job promotion to be a finisher.

After he got sober again, he regained his confidence and his drive to succeed. He had the day off on Tuesday. When he went back to work on Wednesday, his supervisor, Lowell Smith, told him that he was being transferred to the hydrapulper machine so that he could earn more money. When Steve got home, he told me that he didn't want to work the hydrapulper because it was a nasty job that was more difficult and dangerous. His hours changed too. He had to work weekends on the hydrapulper. But he was the type of guy who would do what he was told. He loved his job. All he wanted was to be a finisher.

Steve said the hydrapulper room was horrible because the area was sweltering hot, dirty, and basically disgusting. He told me that the room was used for creating paper pulp by mixing very hot water and newspapers and cardboard in a big underground mixing machine. Steve told me that the machine was dangerous because it was so slippery around the feed hole and all they had was a cable in front of the hole. He said that they assigned him to the hydrapulper and all he was shown was "this damn safety video and some kind of safety pamphlet." Steve said that they really did not train him on how to use the machine properly. Steve understood that the manufacturer of the hydrapulper was responsible for the safety video.

A few days before he died, during one of his first days working on the hydrapulper, Steve told me that a coworker's forklift broke down and Steve had to help the coworker manually feed loose paper into the feed hole. Steve told me that it seemed it was a normal practice based on what his coworker told him. Steve said that there were no warnings around the hydrapulper and that he believed that if something was important enough from a safety perspective, he would have been told about it or there would have been posted warnings relating to anything dangerous. He had only been working on the hydrapulper for a few days before he died.

On the day that he died, I was working at St. Catherine's, and I received a call from Lowell Smith. He told me that there had been a terrible accident and that Steve had fallen into the hole in hydrapulper. He told me that the hole was filled with scalding hot water, so Steve was burned very badly. I was later told by one of Steve's coworkers that they tried to pull him out of the hole, but his skin came off of him and they had to pull him out by his belt. He also told me that they looked for some kind of lifesaver to throw to him, but there was nothing around.

Lowell also told me that they called the ambulance and that he was taken to Nita City Hospital. I asked him if he was still alive, and he said that he was. They told me that Steve was conscious and in a lot of pain when they pulled him out of that dreadful hydrapulper machine that was made by a company named SuperPulper.

I immediately left work and went right to the hospital. I was a complete wreck, and I don't even know how I could drive there. When I got to the hospital, he looked frightening. His skin was red everywhere, and I saw where his skin had come off. It looked like he had been cooked like a lobster. I almost fainted. I immediately grabbed his hand, and he squeezed it back. His eyes were closed, but I asked him to blink his eyes if he knew that it was me, and he did. I asked him to squeeze my hand if he was in pain, and he squeezed my hand again. I know it was a reaction to what I asked him, but I do admit that there were times that he just squeezed my hand without being prompted. I stayed with him all night. He suffered horribly. I did not have my kids come and see him because they were too young and it was just such a scary sight.

I kept asking the nurses and doctors how he was doing, and they kept saying that they didn't know if he would make it because he was burned over 80 percent of his body. They said that they were trying to keep him comfortable with drugs. They never told me whether he was feeling any pain. Every time that I asked them that, the nurses said that they didn't know, and the doctors avoided the issue. They asked me if he had a living will. I told them they he did, and he did not want extraordinary means used to keep him alive. His eyes remained closed all night, but he did keep responding to my questions by squeezing my hand. He never actually talked to me. On the following day, we just watched and waited, and he passed away that day. I was with him when he died. I never left the hospital from the time that I got there until he died.

My kids still cannot believe that their father is gone. They talk about him all the time. I am constantly showing them pictures because they want to remember what their dad looked like. Stevie likes to write his father letters, and when he is done, we read them out loud so Steve can hear them in heaven. As I told you before, Steve was a great dad. He worked a lot, but was always with our family when he wasn't working. He was Stevie's little league coach.

He was an Alderman in our church and also sang in the church choir. The only thing that he did for himself was go bowling once a week. Steve was a role model for our children. We could always count on him to provide helpful guidance to our family.

He was a wonderful husband and was there for me emotionally. We used to talk about how he wanted to make sure that we had enough money so we could pay for our kids' education. We had dreams that our kids would go to college because neither one of us went to college. We wanted a better life for them. That is no longer a reality because I am working just trying to survive. I will have to take out a lot of loans to pay for college. Unfortunately, Steve never bought any life insurance because we couldn't afford it. He said that he would be able to take care of us forever because he would continue to work. Now he is gone and I feel helpless. It's just not right that Steve died the way that he did.

Robin Powell

Robin Powell
Dated: April 11, 2015

Deposition of Lou Petrucelli

My name is Lou Petrucelli. I live at 807 North 21st Street in Nita City, Nita. I am forty-three years old. I have a wife, Suzanne, and two kids, Louis Jr. and Nicole. I graduated high school twenty-five years ago. I did well in school, especially in math and science, and got mostly As and Bs. I've always loved building things and putting things together, so before I graduated, I worked as an auto mechanic for my buddy at Dan's Auto Garage. I was a great mechanic, but I knew as soon as I finished school, I had to work for my father's construction company.

After a few years of working with my father, I knew it wasn't for me. I wanted to get back into a career as a mechanic. One of my buddies, Gregg White, had just landed a job at a company called SuperPulper, Inc., that designed, manufactured, and sold machines called hydrapulpers. I was in the right place at the right time when he got me an interview. It was 1994, and the company's new design engineer, Marc Donaldson, had just been promoted and was looking for help designing new, more efficient hydrapulper models.

From the day I started working at SuperPulper, I really liked my job. It was a little intimidating working with Marc because he was an engineer and I was only a high school graduate, but the machine itself is actually pretty simple. It's just a big mixing bowl that churns paper until it becomes hot paper pulp. It isn't much more complicated than a lawnmower, and I had a lot of experience working with all types of engines already, so I held my own as Marc's assistant. He was the brains, and I was the hands of the operation. He'd design a new model, and then I'd test it out once it was finished to make sure that it worked properly and safely. I'd also go out to different paper manufacturing plants to oversee installations and for follow-up visits. After working under Marc for about six years, he promoted me to Director of Quality Control. As director, it was my job to inspect every hydrapulper that we designed to make sure that it was safe and ready to go to the plants.

I'd only been in my new position for about a year when we got the order from Giant Paper for a new hydrapulper. Marc was all about pleasing the customer, so when Giant Paper asked for a hydrapulper to increase their productivity, that's exactly what they got. Marc and I usually agreed on all of his machine designs, but with this particular model, I had my doubts. During my testing of Hydrapulper 603, I noticed a few issues. If too much paper was pushed in at one time, the auger at the bottom of the machine wouldn't be able to pull it all down. The bundles of paper would then stay afloat and block new paper deposits from being incorporated into the mix. This concerned me because a worker could potentially keep dumping new bales of paper into the machine, backing it up, and unblocking the machine could be dangerous. The auger was also moving too fast at times, causing the hot paper mix to pool around the edges of the machine. This created a slippery mix of hot water and wet paper on the floor near where the operators would be working. With only an eight foot long cable to separate a worker from the machine, I was worried someone could slip. SuperPulper knew that a hydrapulper used in certain environments created this kind of condition around the feedhole.

A manufacturer like SuperPulper understood the industry has this "look busy" culture when a forklift was inoperable. What I mean by that is that based on my training and experience in the field, it's reasonably understood in the industry that workers should look busy in paper pulper plants. Therefore, while workers should appreciate the fact that manually feeding a pulper is potentially dangerous, from my point of view, it's reasonably foreseeable that they could engage in that type of work practice. I tried to raise these issues to Marc a few times during the design process, but he dismissed me. He insisted that as long as workers used the forklifts to feed the machine, which was the intended use, from his point of view it would be efficient and safe. This was only my first year as Director of Quality Control, and I didn't want to rock the boat, so I didn't push the issue. We'd never had a disagreement before, and Marc was still my boss, so I dropped it and we went ahead with the installation.

In the contract for the sale of Hydrapulper 603 between SuperPulper and Giant Paper, the clause regarding the machine's installation indicated a delivery date and a follow-up visit date so that SuperPulper could ensure the machine was working properly. There was also an agreement between the two companies that a customer safety liaison would visit Giant Paper annually to conduct safety seminars and to educate employees about how to use the hydrapulper safely. I was present for the installation, the follow-up, and the first safety seminar at Giant Paper. All workers, regardless of their position, were required to watch an instructional safety video and read a safety pamphlet. Even after all of that went smoothly, I was still concerned. I tried to talk to Marc again, but it was no use. He kept telling me that he believed all of the workers were trained and that the video even included a line about staying away from the hole, and that was the end of it. I saw the video, too, and heard that line, but I didn't think that was enough.

That was also the end of my job as Director of Quality Control. Shortly after the installation at Giant Paper, I was fired. Marc said it was because I'd been "getting lazy" since my promotion, but I think he just didn't like people disagreeing with him. I wasn't even angry. The idea of leaving actually suited me just fine. I didn't want to have anything on my conscience if something went wrong with any of those machines. And from what I heard, things did go wrong after I left. Even though there weren't any specific complaints about Hydrapulper 603, I remember around 2010 or 2011 there were several lawsuits settled out of court. SuperPulper had to pay a considerable amount of money stemming from safety issues with hydrapulpers. All this time, management thought the cable was sufficient to guard against someone falling in, just like they thought no one would be stupid enough to get close to the hole, so they never installed a warning sign. Since no one had ever actually fallen in, I guess they didn't think they needed one.

After I left SuperPulper in 2001 I went to work for a different design engineer. I enjoy what I do, and I'm glad I got out of there when I did.

Lou Petrucelli

Lou Petrucelli
Date: April 11, 2015

David Taylor
5827 Washington Avenue
Nita City, Nita 99908

June 15, 2015

3320 Market Street

Nita City, Nita 99909

Re: Powell v. SuperPulper, Inc.

Dear Mr. Roseman,

I have reviewed the documents that your office supplied regarding the subject case, including the depositions of Robin Powell, Lou Petrucelli, Mark Donaldson, and Lowell Smith, as well as the various photos, animations, and exhibits relating to this case. I have also inspected the hydrapulper that is at issue in this case, which is Hydrapulper 603. I have evaluated the lack of guarding near the feed hole that led to Mr. Powell's demise while he was working near the hydrapulper at the paper plant, Giant Paper.

My opinions are based on my education, training, and experience relating to the design and installation of industrial guards as well as my experience working on hydraulic machines and in manufacturing plants where rotating turbines were present. I also have experience preparing instructions and warnings for various industrial systems. I have a Bachelors of Science in Mechanical Engineering, and I am licensed as a Professional Engineer. Although I have had limited experience with hydrapulpers, it is a simple mechanism with few moving parts and falls well within my expertise in mechanical engineering and safety design.

Incident Description

On July 9, 2013, Steve Powell was working Hydrapulper 603 at a facility known as Giant Paper, located in Nita City. Giant Paper is one of the world's leading manufacturers of corrugated box paper. Just before the accident that killed him, Mr. Powell was assigned to Hydrapulper 603. He had never worked on a hydrapulper before. Hydrapulper 603 is an approximately twenty-foot-diameter by ten- foot-deep vat that mixes waste paper with hot water and sodium hydroxide to cook the mix and make paper pulp. The hydrapulper sits in the basement of the plant, and the opening to the hydrapulper is a large hole in the floor. Both baled and loose papers are fed into the hole. The hole is surrounded by a wide guardrail, except on the feed side, which is an approximately eight-foot-wide opening where paper is at times pushed into the hydrapulper from level with a forklift. Only a cable is used in front of the feed side to act like a guard. There is no guard to prevent accidental entry into the feed hole.

On the day that Mr. Powell fell into the vat, the single-cable rope was draped across the feed side of the hydrapulper. Someone heard Mr. Powell yelling for help, and they found him submerged up to his neck in the mixture of hot water, soda ash, and paper. He was conscious and was pulled from the hydrapulper, transported to the hospital, and died the next day.

Background Information

Continuous paper manufacturing (industrial paper making) dates back to the early 1800s. The plant where Mr. Powell worked took waste paper and recycled it to make boxboard, such as that used in cereal boxes. This process includes loading a hydrapulper with waste paper products and hot (170 degrees Fahrenheit) water, then mixing and beating it with a large auger or impeller to create pulp. Historical documents show hydrapulpers of various types have been used in the industry, but common to all of them is a wall or barrier around the hydrapulper. The hydrapulper at Giant Paper was designed and manufactured by SuperPulper, Inc., and installed in 2001. Normally, when SuperPulper is involved in the installation of a hydrapulper, a forty-two-inch lip is left above the floor to act as a barrier around the hydrapulper. In this case, however, the hydrapulper was installed without the steel guard in front of the feed hole, making it more efficient for the introduction of the bales of paper, but far more dangerous as well. SuperPulper could have and should have designed a safer feed hole that could help prevent accidents like this while maintaining the productivity to be competitive with other paper plants.

By the time Mr. Powell was assigned to Hydrapulper 603, by operation and use, an accumulation of debris had occurred around the hydrapulper. Mr. Powell likely tried to manually push the paper debris into the hydrapulper either by hand or by broom. He then likely lost his balance on the wet and slippery floor. In sum, because of the lack of adequate warning or proper guarding, Mr. Powell fell into the hot paper pulp.

Discussion

My first exposure to a hydrapulper was a project I worked on in 1992 while at Black Rock Safety design. The job was for a plant that manufactured pulp insulation. Pulp was manufactured by dumping corrugated cardboard in a giant twenty-foot diameter vat and mixing it with hot water and other ingredients. The hydrapulper was surrounded by a steel wall approximately four feet high that protected the operator from falling in. The operator used a forklift to place bales of approximately 400 pounds of waste cardboard onto a lift table that was then raised above the level of the wall and tilted, allowing the cardboard to slide into the hydrapulper. This may be slightly less efficient, but prevents any worker from accidentally falling in. Therefore, having the guard may reduce production of paper products, but the company will still be competitive.

When Steve Powell fell into the hydrapulper, the methods to safely load material in hydrapulpers had been known for many years. SuperPulper failed to design a hydrapulper that would adequately protect the operators by allowing the protection system to degrade to a single cable. Mr. Powell, a new worker on the hydrapulper, worked in an environment that was subject to extreme temperature and humidity conditions, where the floor was wet and slippery, and where debris cluttered the work area. The only thing between him and a vat of 170 degree Fahrenheit water was a single cable, which was clearly inadequate to protect an operator from falling into the hydrapulper. An operator falling into the hydrapulper was a foreseeable event, which could have been avoided by a properly designed guard.

It was also foreseeable that a warning on or around the feed hole was necessary to alert and remind any workers, especially those not accustomed to the hydrapulper, of the extreme danger of the feed hole area. The failure to provide this machine with a warning that told operators to stay clear of the feed hole is another reason Hydrapulper 603 was unreasonably dangerous. Had an adequate guard been in place sufficient in size to only permit the entry of paper stock into the feed hole, and/or had there been a sufficient warning in front of the feed hole, this tragic accident would not have happened.

My opinion is supported by the deposition testimony of Mr. Lowell Smith, Giant Paper's hydrapulper supervisor. I recognize the guard may cause a minor decrease in the rate of paper production, but that does not make the guard unnecessary. Safety must come first.

Conclusions

I conclude, based on a reasonable degree of engineering certainty, that the configuration of the cable at the entrance to Hydrapulper 603 was defective and unreasonably dangerous because it did not adequately protect an operator from falling into the hydrapulper. This foreseeable danger could have been easily eliminated through economically and technically feasible design alternatives like the guard shown in the animation and Exhibits 29 and 30. A guard was subsequently put on Hydrapulper 603 after Mr. Powell's accident.

Furthermore, SuperPulper needed to install a warning sign on top of the hydrapulper to tell the operator how to use it and to warn and/or remind the operator about the hazards of the feed hole and of manually introducing paper stock. An adequate warning would have been particularly useful to Mr. Powell, because he was a new worker on the hydrapulper. The proposed warning is also shown in the animation.

The defense contends that this is an "open and obvious" hazard, and yet it failed to provide workers such as Mr. Powell with adequate protections such as I have summarized in this report. Manufactures cannot delegate the responsibility to safely design their products to employers such as Giant Paper—the manufacturer is ultimately responsible. The manufacturers recognize the realities of the workplace: that many times users of the hydrapulper possess varying degrees of training and experience. However, there is no evidence that Mr. Powell misused the product or assumed the risk of injury. He was also using this product in a foreseeable manner for its intended use, and he was also an intended user of the hydrapulper.

As stated above, these opinions are offered to within a reasonable degree of engineering certainty, and I may choose to supplement this report as additional information becomes available.

Sincerely,

David Taylor

David Taylor, ME

David Taylor, ME
5827 Washington Avenue
Nita City, Nita 99908

Education

- Nita University, Nita City, 1975
  - BS in Mechanical Engineering
- Nita University, Nita City, 1978
  - MS in Safety Engineering

Work Experience

- Axial Impellers Inc., Nita City, 1993–present
  - Director of Risk Management
  - Responsibilities include: Overseeing the design and engineering of impeller safety mechanisms, creating warning labels, creating safety instruction manuals for impellers.
- Black Rock Safety Design, New York, NY, 1992
  - Design Engineer for Industrial Safety Equipment
- Hydraulic Technologies, Boston, MA, 1983
  - Design Engineer for Hydraulic Mechanisms including turbines, lifts, cranes, and presses.
- Ford Automobiles, Safety Research and Development Team, 1978
  - Safety Design Engineer

Certification/ Memberships

- Licensed Safety Engineer
- Member, American Society of Safety Engineers
- Minerva Safety Engineering Design Award

Publications

- Safety in Industrial Work Environments: Nothing is Obvious
- Safety Cables, Color Codes, and Warning Signs: The Simple Approach
- Basic Safety Philosophy Applied to Complex and Critical Systems
- Lowering Center of Gravity to Prevent Automobile Roll-Overs

Kevin Racine, MD
510 Pine Street
Nita City, Nita 99999

June 19, 2015

Andrew J. Roseman, Esquire

1 Market Street
Nita City, Nita 99102

Re: Steven Powell

Dear Mr. Roseman,

At your request, I have reviewed the case of Steven Powell. I have reviewed the various documents you provided, including, but not limited to: all of Steven Powell's medical records, all of the depositions taken in this case, the autopsy report, the autopsy photographs, the EMS report, the discharge summary, and the toxicology report. All my opinions and conclusions herein are to a reasonable degree of medical certainty. My conclusion is that Steven Powell was fully conscious while in the paper pulp on the day of the accident, while the EMS personnel attended to him, and when he was admitted to the hospital.

Mr. Powell was 80 percent submerged in paper pulp at a temperature of approximately 160 degrees Fahrenheit for at least a few minutes and up to ten minutes. No one knows exactly how long he was submerged in the pulp. Mr. Powell was eventually pulled from the hydrapulper by coworkers. Mr. Powell was not seen by any EMS personnel for approximately twenty minutes. Mr. Powell was then taken to the hospital, where he received medical care within accepted standards. My conclusion is that while Mr. Powell was in the paper pulp, he was conscious enough to feel the excruciating pain of second- and third-degree burns, as well as the fear, distress, and mental trauma from the nightmarish scenario.

According to coworkers, they think that prior to the accident Mr. Powell was last seen performing some cleaning work near the area of the opening in the floor where Hydrapulper 603 was located. Mr. Powell was most likely fully awake and conscious when he fell into the hot liquid. The statements made by his coworkers make it clear that Mr. Powell was conscious while in the hot liquid *and after he was removed*. During the time he was in the hot liquid, Mr. Powell would have been aware that he was cooking in this industrial broth and he would have experienced incredible fear and distress in addition to unrelenting, severe pain. Efforts to extricate Mr. Powell from the hydrapulper were complicated in part by the inability of his coworkers to get a grasp on Mr. Powell because his skin was sloughing off as a result of the burns. This would certainly have magnified the pain and suffering sustained by Mr. Powell during this process. The pain, as well as the fear, would have persisted after he was finally removed from the liquid. During the Middle Ages, soldiers would pour boiling hot oil on enemies who were attacking their castle—Steven Powell experienced similar, if not worse, pain when he fell into Hydrapulper 603.

The initial assessment in the emergency room at Nita City Hospital attests to the fact that Mr. Powell was conscious at the time he arrived at the hospital; therefore, he would have continued to experience conscious and significant pain and suffering. At the hospital, efforts were made to attempt to control Mr. Powell's pain with analgesics, sedation, and other interventions such as intubation and mechanical ventilation. It is my opinion that during the first day of admission on July 9, 2013, Mr. Powell would have experienced significant conscious pain and suffering.

The autopsy report and photographs, as well as the Nita City Hospital medical records, including the various burn diagrams, describe Mr. Powell as having sustained burns over approximately 80 percent of his total body surface.

The depth of injury from the hot paper pulp is a function of both the temperature of the liquid and the length of the exposure. The temperature of the paper pulp exceeded 160 degrees Fahrenheit. There is no question that Mr. Powell was in liquid that was hot enough, over a long enough period of time, to cause extensive burns as well as an excruciatingly painful circumstance.

According to Mrs. Powell's deposition, Mr. Powell responded to her questions regarding pain by squeezing her hand and blinking his eyes. Although patients who are intubated and sedated can sometimes have involuntary movements of their extremities, I believe that Mr. Powell's movements were purposeful and in response to inquiries posed by his wife. It is also best to discern consciousness based on whether a patient's pulse rate goes up. If it is elevated, it tends to show that the patient is in pain. According to the medical records, Mr. Powell's heart rate was elevated for a brief time. This is all consistent with conscious pain and suffering.

All of these opinions are provided within a reasonable degree of medical certainty, and I ask that you contact me if you need further information relating to this tragic case.

Sincerely,

Kevin Racine

Kevin Racine, MD

Kevin Racine MD
510 Pine Street
Nita City, Nita 99999

Education & Training

Undergraduate
    Penn State University, BS 1989–1993
Graduate
    Temple University Medical School, MD 1993–1998
Postgraduate
    Nita City Medical Center Pain Management Clinic 1998–2001

Work Experience

Bellevue Hospital Center, New York, NY 2001–2005
    Internship Residence in General Surgery
Bellevue Hospital Center, New York, NY 2005–2006
    Fellowship in Burn Care and Pain Management
Upper Extremity Institute, Philadelphia, PA 2008–2011
Nita City Pain Management Clinic 2011–present

Certification/ Memberships

American Board of Surgery 2006 (Recertified in 2015)
Licensed to Practice General and Trauma Surgery and Critical Care Medicine including Pain Management in:
    Nita
    Pennsylvania
    New York

Publications

"Surgery for Car Accident Victims: When Cars Catch Fire"
"The McDonalds Coffee Case: The Severity of Hot Liquid Burns"
"Burn Degree Simplification: Making Sense of the Rating System"

Teaching Positions/Academic Appointment

Nita Medical School, Nita City 2014–Present
    Adjunct Professor of Pain Medicine

Deposition of Mark Donaldson

My name is Mark Donaldson, and I am presently the design engineer for SuperPulper, Inc. I have been in this position for about twenty years. I started with SuperPulper about twenty-five years ago as a maintenance engineer. Throughout my career, I have designed and supervised the installation of industrial equipment, including hydrapulpers, hydraulic lifts, and impellers. I was responsible for designing Hydrapulper 603, in which Steven Powell was injured at the Giant Paper plant.

I hold a bachelor of science degree in marine engineering from Nita Maritime Academy. I studied fluid mechanics for a few months before entering the Navy. I was an officer in the Navy for four years, where I was in charge of the maintenance and operation of a couple of turbine generators. I developed a high degree of proficiency at maintaining the turbine generators, and I started designing new ways to increase productivity and efficiency. This became my specialty. About six months after I left the Navy, I started working at SuperPulper to help increase the productivity of their hydrapulper machines.

Today, I am in charge of the engineering department at SuperPulper. As design engineer, I work directly with the engineers at paper mills, who tell me the needs of their respective companies. I work with them to come up with a design that is consistent with the desires of the company making the order. Usually, the major concerns are safety and productivity. Since I started managing the design department, our sales dramatically increased because I make the most productive and efficient hydrapulpers on the market.

I am also in charge of overseeing the maintenance of SuperPulper hydrapulpers that have been installed in the field. As I said, I was the engineer who designed Hydrapulper 603 at Giant Paper. That hydrapulper was installed in 2001, as I recall. I understand that Steve Powell fell into the hydrapulper on July 9, 2013, because he got too close to the feedhole. After that accident, a steel guard with a chute was installed on that hydrapulper, which prevents access to the area where the paper stock first enters the machine. I could have designed Hydrapulper 603 with such a guard, but it would have minimized the feed hole area, which would inhibit productivity. The single cable guard is the best way to keep the operators safe and maximize paper production. If the hydrapulpers do not make paper efficiently, we cannot compete with foreign paper manufacturers.

The hydrapulper used at Giant Paper is a continuous feed machine. That means that bales of paper stock are regularly loaded through the feeder in the hydrapulper room. This type of hydrapulper doesn't process a set amount of paper stock. Instead, the operators have to monitor the stock inside the hydrapulper and add more as the machine goes through the process. The hydrapulper can process both bales of paper stock and loose waste paper.

The paper production process requires skilled workers in order to operate correctly. But in reality, the users of the hydrapulper possess varying degrees of training and experience. I believe that Mr. Powell was a rewinder at the time. Rewinders do not work near the entrance of the feeder to the hydrapulper. I imagine that Giant Paper also had their rewinders trained to work near the feed hole, too. However, I don't know if Mr. Powell was actually trained to work the hydrapulper. According to his supervisor, Lowell Smith, Mr. Powell had seen the SuperPulper safety video on July 6, 2013.

I checked in with the plant manager frequently to make sure that we didn't need to upgrade any safety devices. But based on Giant Paper's input, and all the positive input we received from all the paper companies who purchased our hydrapulpers, we feel strongly that the cable guard is the best safety mechanism available and it will not unduly hamper production.

After Mr. Powell's accident, Giant Paper made a decision to modify and extend the railings on the side of the feeder entrance to limit employee access. I designed and installed the modification to the feeder entrance myself a few months after Mr. Powell's accident. This turned the area in front of the hydrapulper into a tapered chute, so that bales of paper would be channeled directly in front of the hydrapulper. Before this change, the feeder entrance was about eight feet wide, with a cable in front to stop the forklifts from falling in. The tapered chute is a little more than five feet wide, which was the width of a normal sized bale of paper. The more narrow the chute, the easier it is to jam, which can also be a safety hazard. We could have designed and installed this guard before Steve's accident, but such a design was never requested by a single customer. It's possible that with the guard, the hydrapulper may be safer today than it was on the day of Steve's accident. With that said, it is also my opinion that when the hydrapulper just had the cable and no guard, the hydrapulper was still safe. In fact, in all my years designing hydrapulpers, I can't recall a single safety complaint.

When the hydrapulper was in operation, the operators were supposed to use a forklift to push bales of paper into the feeder entrance, so it would be difficult for workers to get to the opening anyway. The new guard makes it a lot harder to get too close to the feeder entrance. I would also add that the hydrapulper operator doesn't need to get close to the feeder entrance, regardless of whether a chute or cable is used. The operator uses the forklift to push bales of paper into the feeder entrance.

Obviously, it was unfortunate that Steve's accident happened. To this day, no one knows exactly why Steve was so close to the entrance, and no one will ever know without speculating. No part of the hydrapulper operator's job requires him to be so close to the feeder hole. There weren't any warning signs telling people not to get too close to the entrance because of the obvious danger posed by a vat of churning 180 degree Fahrenheit water. I didn't incorporate a warning sign into my design, because common sense indicates that getting too close is dangerous.

Today, the hydrapulper at Giant Paper is less efficient than it was before the new guard was installed. In addition to limiting access, the guard actually makes it harder for the hydrapulper to be used. The cable that was in front of the opening would stop forklifts from going too far and would serve as a reminder to stay back. The wide opening also allowed the forklift to push bales in from different angles. Not all of the bales are the same size, so having a wider feeder entrance increases the number of ways that paper stock can be efficiently loaded into the hydrapulper.

I read the one portion of Lou Petrucelli's deposition relating to the "look busy" conversation that he said he previously had with me, but I don't remember that conversation. While I admit that a properly designed guard to limit access is economically feasible, it nonetheless requires more effort on the part of the worker to keep up with the production demands because the paper bales can jam up. I do admit that I have no studies or evaluations that would show that Giant Paper would be unable to successfully compete in the marketplace if a different access limited guard had been installed.

After Steve's accident, I think the owners of Giant Paper decided that it had to do more to ensure that these types of accidents would be prevented in the future. I suppose that Giant Paper thinks that they have to make these pulpers "idiot proof."

Mark Donaldson

Mark Donaldson

April 14, 2015

Deposition of Lowell Smith

My name is Lowell Smith, and I live at 1500 Arch Street, in Nita City, Nita. I am fifty years old. After I graduated from Nita High School, I went to Nita City Community College for a year and realized that college wasn't for me. When I was done with college, I got a job working at the Samson Paper Company. I was there for over ten years in a lot of different positions. When that company went out of business, I started working for Giant Paper in 1999. Giant Paper is very similar to Samson Paper Company. For the past six years, I have been the supervisor in charge of Giant Paper's hydrapulper machine. I have supervised several employees who operated this machine. One of them was Steve Powell.

I knew Steve Powell for a long time. He began working at Sampson Paper Company around 1998, about a year or two before it went out of business. He came over to Giant Paper a few years after me; I think it was 2000. At Giant Paper, I've only worked on the hydrapulper machines. As the supervisor, I basically supervise the workers on Hydrapulpers 603 and 604 that are located in what is known as the beater room. This room is in the basement of the plant. Steve's accident happened in the "beater room," where the pulp first goes into the machine. I think Steve had only been working in the beater room for a few days before the accident.

The beater room is basically where the process begins—it is like a big mixing bowl. The pulping machine has a rotor at the bottom that chops everything up and mixes it all together. After the beater room, this paper pulp mixture gets dried and processed into paper. I think Steve usually worked as a rewinder, which is not in the beater room. That job is closer to the end of the process of making paper. I admit that the room where the rewinder machines are is not as dirty, hot, and slippery as the beater room.

I know that when the hydrapulper was installed, there was a representative of the Manufacturer, SuperPulper, present to give us instructions on how to use the hydrapulper with a video. He also gave us a safety pamphlet. I do remember a statement in the video about staying away from the feed hole; unfortunately, preoccupied workers don't always follow that warning.

When Steve started working in the beater room, I showed him SuperPulper's safety video before he started using Hydrapulper 603 and gave him the safety pamphlet. The representative from SuperPulper told me that showing the safety video was sufficient to train the beater room employees in order for them to safely use the hydrapulper.

Truthfully, I'm not exactly sure why Steve was transferred to the beater room. I think a lot of people in the plant want to be finishers, which is what Steve wanted to do. It is a much cleaner job and pays more. The beater room is one of the harder jobs, and it's actually a downgrade from some positions. Let's face it, working the beater room was a dirty, nasty, and dangerous job, but the pay was pretty good, and it paid better than what a rewinder earned.

About two weeks before Steve's accident, another employee had slipped and fallen on some oil and water in the machine room area. This is a different area than where Steve's accident happened. Because of that other accident, I held a meeting with my crew to discuss safety issues, like being aware of your surroundings and avoiding injuries. Steve was at that meeting and asked some basic questions about hydrapulper operations and safety procedures. This meeting took place after Steve saw the safety video. I guess that video didn't really sink in. Steve was asking some basic stuff. I didn't have much time to cover a lot of the details of his questions. It was pretty obvious that Steve was a "rookie" when it came to proper operating procedures. However, again, I told Steve to refer to SuperPulper's safety video and pamphlet because SuperPulper maintained that their video and pamphlet were sufficient to explain how to work the machine safely.

On the day of Steve's accident, he was the hydrapulper operator of 603 in the beater room. The hydrapulper operator uses a forklift to push bales of paper into the machine. The forklift would go onto a platform that led to the entrance of the hydrapulper. At the entrance, there was a cable so the forklift wouldn't fall in.

On that day, I remember that the guy working before Steve had some issues with the forklift and wanted me to take a look. Because we were looking at the forklift, Steve obviously couldn't use it. No more paper was supposed to be loaded in until we fixed the issue with the forklift. So I was working on the forklift near the number 604 hydrapulper, which is also relatively close to Hydrapulper 603.

The way the machine works is that it takes a certain amount of paper stock, which is added by the hydrapulper operator. After the stock is added, the stock gets thicker as it mixes with the hot water. It can get pretty messy and slippery where the stock is added because there's a lot of water. On the day of the accident, July 9, 2013, I didn't see what Steve was doing. But he was most likely adding loose paper to the feed hole by using a broom or by hand, and he may have slipped in. There were no witnesses, and I really don't know how the accident occurred. However, after the accident, I did see a broom on the ground near the entrance to the vat.

Anyway, while I was working on the forklift near the number 604 hydrapulper, I heard a faint voice near the 603 pulper. It sounded like someone was calling my name, but I wasn't sure because it's so damn loud in the beater room. After a while, I heard the same sound. That's when I looked over, and I couldn't see who was operating Hydrapulper 603. I walked over to the operator's control panel, and that's when I saw Steve moving around inside the hydrapulper. I don't know what happened or how long he was in there, and I couldn't believe my eyes.

I called for help and ran over to try to pull him out. I had to use the cable that was there to keep myself from falling in. I was able to grab onto his arm, but I couldn't pull him out myself. His skin was starting to come off, and I had to grab onto his belt. After a few minutes, several people came to help, and we were able to pull Steve out. He kept saying, "I'm hot. I'm hot. I feel like I am on fire." It would have been helpful if there had been some retrieval equipment, but there was nothing available at the time; however, due to the thickness of the stock, I'm not sure how much it would have helped.

We don't have any doctors that work at the paper mill, but someone called the paramedics. After about twenty minutes the paramedics showed up. All we could do was try to keep him comfortable until they came. We ripped off his shirt and put some water on top of him to try to keep him cool. We aren't medical people, but we did the best we could for him. The paramedics came and took Steve to the hospital.

At the hospital, Steve's wife Robin was there. I didn't see either one of their kids. The doctors only allowed me to see him for a few minutes. He was alive, but the doctors told me that he was sedated to help keep his pain level down. His skin was really red. His eyes were closed and his face looked like it was swelling up. The next time I saw Steve was at the funeral.

Right after Steve's accident, the superintendent and the assistant superintendent got all the workers together in the office. They wanted to make sure that everyone was OK, and they said we could leave for the day if we wanted. A lot of us took the rest of the day off to go see Steve at the hospital.

We had a safety meeting a few days later. I don't remember if it was only about Steve's accident, but we did talk about making the hydrapulper safer. We talked about putting a steel guard in front of the feed hole to the hydrapulper. A lot of guys asked why the manufacturer didn't provide that type of guard when SuperPulper sold the machine to Giant Paper. I also remember a few workers voicing complaints to management asking why Giant Paper didn't retrofit the hydrapulper with a guard. And I remember the more experienced operators saying that a guard would unnecessarily slow down production. I also heard some people question why Steve got so close to the feed hole. Management told us that SuperPulper told them that their design engineer, Mark Donaldson, suggested that a steel guard would inhibit productivity. We found out that there was nothing wrong with the hydrapulper machine. It did not malfunction or anything and never had any maintenance issues.

The hydrapulper today has a steel guard that feeds into the entrance so that no one can get too close. The operators aren't supposed to get close to the entrance to feed stock into the machine anyway, but I guess the new guard makes it impossible for them to get all the way up there. We also now have a written warning to tell hydrapulper operators how to correctly use the machine and to stay away from the opening. I'm not sure why that warning is there because it is obvious that an operator should stay away from the hole. I am not convinced that the steel guard makes things safer for anyone working on the hydrapulper who properly uses a forklift. But I do admit that since the guard was put in place we have not had any further accidents, but sometimes it jams up. That guard reduces our output volume of paper product. I have to say that Steve was a great worker and a terrific guy. Sometimes I would have lunch with him, and a few times my wife and I had dinner with Steve and his wife Robin. Steve was known to sometimes have a few too many beers. I don't think that he was ever drinking on the job, but I guess anything is possible. I do recall that there was an incident when Steve could not be found while he was on the clock, but I forget the exact details. A formal report was written about it.

I have never heard people refer to the "look busy" culture in a paper mill, but superiors give better performance reviews to workers who display a consistent, hard-working attitude while they are on the clock.

I have to admit that I was convicted of a crime five years ago, but it was not a big deal. I took a pinball machine from someone's basement because my son was gravely ill and all he wanted was a pinball machine, and I couldn't afford to buy one. This conviction was for felony theft, and I received two years of probation and had to do community service. I am very regretful for what I did. Thank God, my son is fine now!

Lowell Smith

Lowell Smith

April 14, 2015

Sarah Tower, PhD
Massachusetts Institute of Technology
77 Massachusetts Avenue
Cambridge, MA 02139

June 18, 2015

Re: Powell v. SuperPulper, Inc.

Dear Ms. Sheppard:

As you requested, I have reviewed the depositions of Robin Powell, Lou Petrucelli, Mark Donaldson, and Lowell Smith; the SuperPulper's safety video; various photos; the animation; and exhibits relating to this case. I also inspected the SuperPulper Hydrapulper 603 after the accident. The purpose of my report is to offer my objective opinion as to whether the SuperPulper hydrapulper in question was "defective." Further, if defective, whether that alleged defect in Hydrapulper 603 was the cause of Mr. Powell's injuries and death. Based on all the materials I personally reviewed, and my expertise in the field of mechanical engineering and safety, I conclude that 1) the hydrapulper was not defective; 2) it did not cause any injury to Mr. Powell; 3) the hydrapulper did not require written warnings because the danger was open and obvious; and 4) Mr. Powell assumed the risk, and unfortunately, he was the cause of his own injuries and death.

I am a mechanical and design engineer and graduated from Georgia Institute of Technology in 1994. I started working in the hydrapulper industry in 1996. I have specifically worked on the safety and design of impellers, the propeller-shaped rotating blade used on machines like hydrapulpers. Hydrapulpers, like the one in this case, are large centrifuges filled with hot liquid, with an impeller at the base, where recycled paper is churned to make a liquid-paper pulp used for various purposes.

The hydrapulper involved in this case was located below floor level in a section of the paper mill used to prepare paper pulp. Large bales of paper, along with some loose waste paper, were supposed to be efficiently and safely introduced into the feed hole by use of a forklift. It was not an accepted practice at the paper mill to attempt to introduce stock into the hydrapulper manually, primarily because it would require the operator to be in dangerous proximity to the opening. After the paper stock was properly introduced into the feed hole, the stock fell by gravity through the large hole located in the floor and into the hydrapulper. Except for the entrance, where the paper was introduced by machine into the hydrapulper, the hydrapulper was guarded on all sides by beams, which formed a protective railing. At the mouth of the feed hole, the entrance was guarded with a cable about eight feet from the edge of the floor opening.

The cable also serves as a warning, confirming that which is obvious—stay away from the feed hole! Also, the safety video sufficiently warned workers of safety issues with this product and warned the workers to stay away from the feed hole. Of course, if someone such as Mr. Powell choose to disregard the warning and got too close to the feed hole, he assumed the risk of injury. It is common knowledge to anyone whose job is feeding the hydrapulper that the feed hole is dangerous and not to get too close.

I admit that many floor-fed hydrapulpers are guarded on all sides with beams and a metal chute that will definitely prevent someone from falling in the hole. However, those designs are typically used for smaller scale operations where the paper bales are fed by hand, without the aid of a forklift.

Hydrapulper 603 typically handled paper bales that weighed more than 1,000 pounds, and had to be pushed into the hydrapulper by the use of a forklift. Therefore, it is unforeseeable (and unnecessary) that any worker would feed paper by hand into an industrial hydrapulper of that size. Loose paper should never be added to the hydrapulper manually by pushing or sweeping the loose paper through the entrance area and into the hydrapulper. Therefore, the manufacturer, SuperPulper, appropriately recognized that the cable was the most efficient safety measure that enables forklifts to work while preventing forklift operators from falling in the hole and lets workers know that the feed hole was not a safe area.

Anyone observing the rotating mixture of hot water and dissolving paper in the hydrapulper tank below the floor immediately should have known that it was not safe to be anywhere near the edge of the floor opening for any reason. The floor area around the hydrapulper opening was typically wet with water and paper product. Therefore, it should have been apparent to any worker that walking on the floor near the hydrapulper was very dangerous. Regardless of how Mr. Powell fell into the hole, he must have gotten too close to the hole in contrast to common sense.

Regardless of whether or not there was a "look busy" culture or whether or not workers receive more favorable performance reviews by displaying a hard-working attitude in a paper mill, there is no excuse for a worker engaging in an unsafe or dangerous work practice by getting too close to the feed hole.

I do acknowledge that it would have been economically feasible to have a proper access limiting guard, but it would have required the workers to expend more time and energy when the hydrapulper jammed up.

It is my conclusion within a reasonable degree of engineering certainly that: 1) Hydrapulper 603 was safe for its intended use; 2) that Mr. Powell unfortunately assumed the risk of the danger and slipped into the hydrapulper tank, thereby causing his own injuries; and 3) that the steel cable that was in plain sight was a sufficient safety warning.

Yours truly,

Sarah Tower

Sarah Tower, PhD

Sarah Tower, PhD
Massachusetts Institute of Technology
77 Massachusetts Avenue
Cambridge, MA 02139

Education

- Georgia Technical Institute, 1994
    - BS in Mechanical Engineering
    - Minor in Fluid Mechanics
- California Institute of Technology, Pasadena, CA 1996
    - MS in Molecular Engineering
    - Thesis: "Carbon Construction: The Buckminsterfullerene"
- Massachusetts Institute of Technology, Cambridge, MA 2001
    - PhD in Mechanical Engineering
    - Thesis: "Complex Industrial Propeller Induced Systems in the Workforce"

Work Experience

- Massachusetts Institute of Technology, Cambridge, MA 1999–Present
    - Professor in Mechanical Engineering
    - Consultant on Safety Engineering
    - Scholarship Focusing on Safety Engineering
- Acushnet Company, Fairhaven, MA 1996–1999
    - Design Engineer
    - Polymer Research and Development

Certification/ Memberships

- Member, American Society of Safety Engineers
- Licensed Professional Engineer 2000 (US 33189)

Publications

- "Lighter and Stronger: The Utility of Titanium in Golf Club Manufacturing" 1998
- "Elastomers: The New World of Golf Ball Production Without Adversely Affecting Utility" 1999
- "Bright Cable Warnings: Apparent Safety Warnings in the Industrial Workforce" 2006

Thornton D. Wentworth, MD
Burn Care Foundation
111 Old York Road
Cambridge, MA 02138

June 22, 2015

Re: Steve Powell, deceased

Dear Ms. Sheppard,

You have asked me to review the records of Steve Powell, who fell into Hydrapulper 603 at the Giant Paper mill on July 9, 2013. You have also asked me to offer my opinions relating to the extent of Mr. Powell's injuries and whether he experienced conscious pain and suffering as a result of his accident. For the purpose of this report, I have reviewed Mr. Powell's EMS records, medical records from the Nita City Hospital, autopsy photographs, and all of the deposition transcripts. All of the opinions I express in this report are held to a reasonable degree of medical certainty. My opinion is that while this accident was incredibly tragic, Mr. Powell fortunately only experienced a very brief episode of conscious pain and suffering, and he was exposed to the hot paper pulp for a relatively short period of time.

Although not intended, it appears that most of the damage to Mr. Powell's skin occurred secondary to the workers attempting to pull Mr. Powell from the hydrapulper and not his exposure to the hot pulp. (I understand that, unfortunately, sufficient worker retrieval methods did not exist at the paper mill). In any event, the records of Giant Paper show that the temperature of the paper stock inside the hydrapulper falls somewhere between 140 and 180 degrees Fahrenheit. These temperatures are sufficient to cause full thickness burns, or third degree burns, when one is exposed after an extensive period of time (two minutes or more). Moreover, in the time period that one would be exposed to these temperatures, it is highly unlikely that a human being would be capable of experiencing conscious pain and suffering for anything in excess of a few minutes before becoming unconscious or semi-conscious in light of the extensive pain. Because Mr. Powell was conscious when being pulled from the hot liquid, I conclude that he could not have been in the hot paper pulp for more than a few minutes.

The EMS report states that at least twenty minutes passed from when they were dispatched until Mr. Powell was taken to the hospital. The EMS report does say that Mr. Powell was somewhat conscious when he was put in the ambulance. However, the deposition testimony suggests that Mr. Powell was not fully conscious, but going in and out of consciousness. This means that Mr. Powell likely did not feel pain and suffering of a fully conscious adult.

Although Mr. Powell was able to survive these injuries temporarily, I agree with the plaintiff's expert that the hospital provided care that was within acceptable standards in the medical community. In fact, the hospital staff did an excellent job of controlling Mr. Powell's pain. By successfully treating Mr. Powell with analgesics and sedatives, the hospital staff was able to control and minimize any potential pain Mr. Powell was experiencing when admitted.

Sedatives and analgesics can cause involuntary extremity movements. I understand that Mrs. Powell has testified that she believes that Mr. Powell was responding to her conversation with him while his eyes were closed. Those were probably involuntary, non-purposeful motions that patients may experience in a reduced conscious state or while a patient is in a coma. This can also happen when a patient is intubated. This is not evidence of conscious pain and suffering.

My conclusion is that Mr. Powell could not have experienced full conscious pain and suffering during his hospital stay before he died. A reliable factor to show if a patient is experiencing pain is to see whether a burn patient has an elevated heart rate and Mr. Powell only had an elevated heart rate when he entered the hospital. Once he was intubated and sedated, his heart rate went back to normal, indicating the absence of conscious pain.

It has been my experience as a burn specialist that an individual who has suffered burns such as Mr. Powell's would have been conscious for only a very brief period of time. In addition, patients such as Mr. Powell would have extensive nerve damage associated with third-degree burns. Third-degree burns actually reduce the extent to which one can appreciate pain because once the nerve receptors die, pain can no longer be felt. It is my conclusion that Mr. Powell's burns were third degree and not second degree, which would have been more painful.

I have also reviewed the autopsy photographs, which depict Mr. Powell with severe burns over almost 80 percent of his body. Mr. Powell's head, neck, and hands were generally uninjured, because those areas were not immersed in the paper stock. The photographs are very inflammatory and offer no helpful medical evidence to prove (or disprove) whether Mr. Powell experienced conscious pain and suffering.

Again, all of these opinions are expressed to a reasonable degree of medical certainty. To the extent that records reviewed are not mentioned or contrary to the views expressed in this report, I have considered them and rejected their conclusions. It should be noted that the plaintiff's expert is a trauma surgeon and not a burn specialist.

Sincerely,

Thornton D. Wentworth

Thornton D. Wentworth, MD

Thornton D. Wentworth, MD
Burn Care Foundation
111 Old York Road
Cambridge, MA 02138

Education & Training

- Undergraduate - Harvard University, BS 1968–1972
- Graduate - Harvard University Medical School, MD 1972–1976
- Postgraduate
    - General Surgery Residency
        - Massachusetts General Hospital 1976–1981
    - Trauma Surgery Fellowship
        - Brigham and Women's Hospital 1981–1983
    - Burn Trauma Critical Care Fellowship
        - Brigham and Women's Burn Center 1993–1995

Work Experience

- Brigham and Women's Hospital
    - Chief Attending Trauma Surgeon and Director of Critical Care 1983–1993
- Massachusetts General Hospital Burn Unit
    - Chief Attending Burn Trauma Surgeon 1995–2011
- Burn Care Foundation
    - President and Founder 2011–Present

Certification/Memberships

- American Board of Trauma Surgeons
    - Member 1985–Present
- Board Certified in General Surgery

Publications

- "The Whining Patient: American's Low Threshold"
- "Computers and Carpel Tunnel Syndrome"
- "Why Second Degree Burns Can Be More Painful"
- "Burns and Loss of Consciousness: How Much Pain is Too Much?"
- "Not All Pain is Bad: Nerves in the Neck."

Jury Instruction—Introduction

(Read by the Judge before Opening of Plaintiff's Case)

As the jury in this case, you will be the judges of the facts, and you will be the only judges of the facts. You will have to decide what happened. I play no part in judging the facts. That is your responsibility.

My role is to be the judge of the law; that is to say, I make whatever legal decisions have to be made during the course of the trial, and I will explain to you the legal principles that must guide you in your decisions on the facts.

You are to judge the facts in this case based on the evidence presented to you and based only on the evidence. This evidence will consist of the testimony of witnesses, the exhibits marked into evidence, and any material that we read to you.

As the trier of fact, it will be your job to judge the believability of the witnesses. Size up the witness. Is the witness telling the truth? Does the witness know what he/she is talking about? How good is the witness's recollection? Is the witness accurate and correct in what he/she is saying? You may also consider the demeanor of the witness; that is, how is the witness behaving and responding to the questions asked? You may believe part of the witness's testimony and not believe other parts of it.

At the close of the entire case, I will explain to you the law that applies to this case. You must accept the law as I explain it to you and apply it to the facts as you find them to be based on the evidence.

Jury Instruction—Law

(TO BE READ AFTER CLOSING ARGUMENTS)

The defendant SuperPulper, as the manufacturer or seller of a product, has the duty to make or sell a product that is reasonably safe. By reasonably safe, I mean a product that is reasonably fit, suitable, and safe for its intended or reasonably foreseeable purpose.

The defendant SuperPulper is liable only if plaintiff proves that the hydrapulper causing the harm was not reasonably safe for its intended purpose. In this case, the plaintiff is bringing two separate claims that the hydrapulper was not reasonably safe for its intended purpose because of

A. a design defect; and

B. a failure to adequately warn.

Products Liability—Design Defect

One of the plaintiff's claims against SuperPulper is that Hydrapulper 603 was defectively designed.

1. To prove a design defect existed in the hydrapulper, the plaintiff must have proven that:
    a. the hydrapulper risks outweighed its utility—by this I mean the risks were greater than its intended purpose—or;
    b. that a practical and feasible, safer, alternative design existed that would have reduced or prevented the harm.
2. When determining if a design defect existed on the hydrapulper, you may consider the following factors:
    a. the usefulness and desirability of product aspects;
    b. the safety aspects of the hydrapulper;
    c. availability of substitutes;
    d. ability to eliminate its unsafe characteristics without great expense or impairing usefulness;
    e. user's ability to avoid danger;
    f. user's anticipated awareness of inherent dangers and their avoidability;
    g. feasibility of spreading loss.

Products Liability—Inadequate Warning

The plaintiff's other claim against SuperPulper is that Hydrapulper 603 contained inadequate warnings.

With respect to that claim, SuperPulper, as the manufacturer or seller of a product, has a nondelegable duty to provide adequate warnings about the potential dangers of the hydrapulper.

SuperPulper had this duty even if the hydrapulper was perfectly designed and manufactured. When addressing the plaintiff's failure to warn claim, you must determine what warnings the defendant provided and whether those warnings and instructions were adequate

To be adequate, the warning must be the kind of warning of which a reasonably prudent manufacturer or seller in the same or similar circumstances would have provided to the people intended to use the product.

An adequate warning will communicate sufficient information on the dangers of the product and how to use the product safely. You must also take into account the ordinary knowledge common to the anticipated user of the hydrapulper.

The plaintiff is required to prove that the absence of a warning was a proximate cause of his harm, and there is a rebuttable presumption that a plaintiff would have heeded the warning.

An adequate warning is evaluated in terms of what SuperPulper knew at the time it produced the hydrapulper and what they should have known based on reasonably available information.

Affirmative Defense

SuperPulper seeks to establish that Steven Powell assumed the risk from the danger the plaintiff contends caused Steven Powell's death. Therefore, it is SuperPulper's burden of proof to show that defense.

In order to establish that Steven Powell assumed the risk, SuperPulper must prove, by a preponderance of the evidence, the following elements:

1. that the plaintiff had actual knowledge of the risk;
2. that the plaintiff fully appreciated the dangers resulting from the risk; and
3. that he knowingly and voluntarily exposed himself to the danger.

If you find that SuperPulper has proven all of these elements, then the defendant has met its burden of proof to establish the defense of assumption of the risk. If, on the other hand, you decide that SuperPulper has failed to prove any of these elements by a preponderance of the evidence, then you may not consider assumption of the risk as a defense in this matter.

Damages

I shall now instruct you on the law governing damages in the event that you decide the liability issue in favor of the plaintiff. The fact that I instruct you on damages should not be considered as suggesting any view of mine one way or the other about which party is entitled to prevail in this case. In cases like this one, there may be many claims for damages. However, in this case, you are required to only address one claim for damage. More specifically, you must address the plaintiff's claim for Steven Powell's conscious pain and suffering.

Damages for pain and suffering are compensatory for any pain, discomfort, fear, anxiety, and other mental and emotional distress suffered by plaintiff's decedent. There is no definite standard or method of calculation to determine reasonable compensation for pain and suffering.

Again, I am required by law to give this instruction regarding damages; it in no way indicates I have an opinion about the liability of a party in this case.

Summary

The Court did not, and does not by these instructions, offer any opinions as to what has or has not been proven in a case. Your oath as jurors requires you to decide this case fairly and impartially, without sympathy, passion, bias, or prejudice. You are to decide this case based solely on the evidence that you find believable and in accordance with the rules of law that I give you.

The plaintiff, and in certain defenses as I instructed you earlier, the defendant's burden of proof in this case is the preponderance of the evidence. By this I mean that so long as you find that the scales tip, however slightly, in favor of the plaintiff, they have met their burden of proof. If you find that the plaintiff has shown by the preponderance of the credible evidence that:

1. the product had a design defect or inadequate warning, as I previously described, in that it was not reasonably safe for its intended or reasonably foreseeable uses;
2. the defect existed when the product left the hands and control of the defendant;
3. that the defect caused injury to a direct or reasonably foreseeable user or to a person who might reasonably be expected to come into contact with the product; and
4. that the defect in the product was a proximate cause of the accident,

then you must find for the plaintiff. Plaintiff is not required to prove that it was the sole cause.

If plaintiff has failed either one or both of these claims that I previously described, then you must find for the defendant.

IN THE UNITED STATES DISTRICT COURT
FOR THE DISTRICT OF NITA

Robin Powell, Individually and as Administratrix of the Estate of Steven Powell, Decedent,	:	
	:	CIVIL ACTION
Plaintiff	:	
	:	9-2015
v.	:	
SuperPulper, Inc.	:	
Defendant	:	

JURY VERDICT FORM (LIABILITY AND DAMAGES)

1. Do you find that Hydrapulper 603 was defectively designed?

_______Yes _______No

If you answered "Yes," please go to question 2. If you answered "No," please go to question 3.

2. Do you find that a defective design in the hydrapulper was a substantial factor in causing Steven Powell's injuries?

_______Yes _______No Please go to question 3.

3. Do you find that the defendant failed to provide an adequate warning relating to the subject hydrapulper?

_______Yes _______No

If you answered "Yes," please go to question 4. If you answered "No" to this question, but you answered "Yes" to questions 1 and 2, please go to 5.

4. Do you find that the defendant's failure to provide an adequate warning relating to the subject hydrapulper was a substantial factor in causing Steven Powell's injuries?

_______Yes _______No

If you answered "Yes," please go to question 5. If you answered "No" to this question, but you answered "Yes" to questions 1 and 2, please go to the next question.

5. State the amount of damages you find in favor of the plaintiff and against the defendant for Steven Powell's pain and suffering.

$ ______________________________

Date: ____________________________

____

FOREPERSON

IN THE UNITED STATES DISTRICT COURT
FOR THE DISTRICT OF NITA

Robin Powell, Individually and as Administratrix of the Estate of Steven Powell, Decedent,	:	
	:	CIVIL ACTION
Plaintiff	:	
	:	9-2015
v.	:	
SuperPulper, Inc.	:	
Defendant	:	

JURY VERDICT FORM (LIABILITY ONLY)

1. Do you find that Hydrapulper 603 was defectively designed?

_______ Yes _______No

If you answered "Yes," please go to question 2. If you answered "No," please go to question 3.

2. Do you find that a defective design in the hydrapulper was a substantial factor in causing Steven Powell's injuries?

_______Yes _______No Please go to question 3.

3. Do you find that the defendant failed to provide an adequate warning relating to the subject hydrapulper?

_______Yes _______No

If you answered "Yes," please go to question 4. If you answered "No" and you have addressed all the questions in this verdict form, please return to the courtroom.

4. Do you find that the defendant's failure to provide an adequate warning relating to the subject hydrapulper was a substantial factor in causing Steven Powell's injuries?

_______Yes _______No

If you have answered "Yes" to questions 1 and 2 and/or questions 3 and 4, you have found in favor of the plaintiff. If you have not found as referenced above, you have found in favor of the defendant. Please return to the courtroom after you have addressed the question in this verdict form.

Date: ______________________________

____

FOREPERSON

Exhibit 1

EXCERPT FROM THE NITA EXAMINER: Monday, July 11, 2013

NITA CITY, NITA: Giant Paper employee Steven Powell died last night as a result of a horrific accident that occurred at the Giant Paper plant earlier this week.

The accident that caused Mr. Powell's injuries and led to his death took place on July 9, when he somehow fell into a machine called a hydrapulper.

A hydrapulper mixes recycled paper product with near-boiling water and other chemicals to produce paper pulp, which is then used to create recycled paper.

According to sources speaking anonymously, Steven fell in the hot paper mixture and was pulled out by his co-workers. He kept saying, "I'm hot! I feel like I'm on fire!"

My reliable sources tell me that they believe Steven was conscious when he was pulled from the hot paper mix. An ambulance was called, and Mr. Powell was rushed to Nita Hospital.

Steven spent two days in the hospital before succumbing to his injuries. He had severe burns over most of his body.

Mr. Powell is survived by his wife and two children.

The case of Steven Powell may be yet another example of the industrial safety reforms needed in Nita City. Mr. Powell's death may have been accidental, but increased safety standards can only improve the work conditions for Nita City employees. With the upcoming mayoral elections, protecting the workers in Nita City should be a top priority.

Exhibit 2

EXCERPT FROM THE NITA EXAMINER: Wednesday July 13, 2013

Obituary: Steven Powell, 34, of Nita City died on July 10, 2013. He is survived by his wife of ten years, Robin Powell, and his two children, Stevie and Sarah.

Steven and Robin met at Upper Dublin High School and were childhood sweethearts. Steve had worked at Giant Paper for the last twelve years and was an active member of the Nita Community.

Steve loved his family. He coached his son Stevie's little league baseball team. You could always find Steve around Nita Park practicing with his young son. He also played an active role in his daughter's life.

Steve loved the Nita community. He was a founding member of the Nita City food bank and was an Alderman in his church. Steve organized the annual Thanksgiving food drive to help support the needy around the holidays.

Steve and Robin moved to Nita from Upper Dublin ten years ago and have been a valuable addition to the community. Steve's contributions to his family, to Giant Paper, and to the entire Nita community will surely be missed.

Please send any contributions to "The Legacy of Steven Powell" at 3400 Market St., Nita City, Nita.

Exhibit 3

Nita City EMS Report

Date: July 9, 2013

Time Pickup: 11:47 a.m.

Pickup Location: Giant Paper, Inc.

Drop-off Time: 11:57 a.m.

Drop-off Location: Nita Hospital

Patient Name: Steven Powell

Age: 34

Sex: M

Chief Complaint/Reason for Transport

I received a radio call at approximately 11:29 a.m. to respond to a paper mill worker who fell into a vat of hot water/paper mix. When I arrived on the scene, the patient was surrounded by coworkers. He was conscious. His coworker said that since being pulled from the hot paper mixture, the patient kept screaming, "I'm hot! I feel like I'm on fire!" I asked Steven what happened and a series of other questions, and he continued to say, "I'm hot." When I asked if he was in pain, he said, "Yes."

When we arrived, his shirt was off, and we took off the patient's remaining clothes. We then wrapped him in a burn blanket. With his coworkers' help, we put him on a gurney and wheeled him out of the boiler room and into the loading dock where the ambulance was parked. There was trash everywhere, which made moving the gurney difficult. The patient experienced severe burns over most of his body.

Vital Signs

Pulse: 150 bpm

Blood Pressure: 180/30

Glucose Levels: Normal

Oxygen Levels: Low

Body Temperature: 104.8°F

Provider's Immediate Concerns

My immediate concern was the patient's burns and his pain level. His burns covered almost his entire body, and without an outer layer of skin to shield off bacteria and disease, his condition could deteriorate.

The patient also had a high fever that should have come down after treatment at the hospital. I gave him analgesics to help with his pain. He was conscious on arrival at the hospital.

J. Morgan

EMS Technician

Date: July 10, 2013

Exhibit 4

NITA CITY HOSPITAL
Discharge Summary

Name: Powell, Stephen

Number: 156-24-05

Date of Admission: July 9, 2013

Date of Discharge: July 10, 2013

Attending Physician: Stanley Jones, MD

Mr. Powell is a 34-year-old African American male. He was brought to the Nita City Hospital Emergency Department by EMT's after he fell into a vat of water/paper mix, which was approximately 160 degrees Fahrenheit. He arrived at the hospital at 11:58 a.m. after being removed from the hot paper mix by coworkers.

On arrival to the emergency department, Mr. Powell had a pulse rate of 150 beats per minute, his blood pressure was 180/30, and his body temperature was 104.3 degrees Fahrenheit. Mr. Powell was resuscitated as per Trauma Protocol and was intubated immediately after resuscitation. An intravenous line via the right femoral vein was placed at the time. He was given Fentanyl for pain, and he was sedated. After approximately one hour of receiving Fentanyl, his pulse rate reduced to 100 beats per minute.

Mr. Powell was evaluated by the physicians from the Burn Team and was admitted to the Burn Unit. He was estimated to have approximately an 80 percent body surface area burn, including second- and third-degree burns. He was brought to the Treatment Room, where his skin was cleaned and excess dead skin was removed. A Foley catheter was placed, and a right femoral arterial line was also placed. His wounds were dressed, and he was placed in his room for continuous cardiac and respiratory monitoring. He was on a ventilator at the time as well.

Next, a basic blood test was performed, revealing a severe clotting problem. At that point, he was determined to be in disseminated intravascular coagulopathy (DIC) and was started with packed red blood cells, fresh frozen plasma, and cryoprecipitate to treat the condition. Labs were sent off again. At that time, a hematology/oncology consult was obtained for additional input regarding treatment.

At this point, Mr. Powell's condition was not yet stable. He was resuscitated with lactated ringers and normal saline fluids. He had multiple episodes with decreased blood pressure and required a dobutamine infusion to maintain his blood pressure. His fluid resuscitation and blood product administration continued into the evening, at which point he started to have decreased urinary output. No urine was obtainable despite the Foley catheter in place. He continued to receive full fluid resuscitation with no urine output due to severe shock. He continued to have a coagulopathy as per his physical exam and his laboratory studies. Once stabilized as stated above, he was on a continuous dosage of Fentanyl throughout the course of his hospitalization until his demise.

On the morning of the July 10, Mr. Powell had become extremely swollen with a very firm chest and abdomen, and a dialysis catheter was placed into his abdomen. However, the pressure in his abdomen was so great that dialysis was ineffective. At that time, another central venous catheter was placed in his right groin for access, and just prior to the initiation of dialysis, his heart rate became extremely slow and eventually stopped. Advanced Cardiac Life Support protocol was initiated, including the administration of Epinephrine, Atropine, Sodium Bicarbonate, Dopamine, CPR, and respiratory management, which was unsuccessful in maintaining an adequate rhythm. At approximately 9:55, with the monitor and two leads showing no heart rate, the code was called and he was pronounced dead. The Fire Marshall was also notified, as was the Medical Examiner as this will be a Medical Examiner case. Family was informed and allowed to see the patient.

Stanly Jones

Stanley Jones, MD, Attending Physician

Date: July 10, 2013

Exhibit 5

REPORT OF MEDICAL EXAMINER
City of Nita
Office of the Medical Examiner

Decedent: Steven Powell

Scalding injury involving about 80% total body skin:

Relative sparing of head and face

Relative sparing of left hand and wrist

Relative sparing of the scrotum

Relative sparing of the gluteal crease

Relative sparing of the soles of the feet

An external examination on the remains of Steven Powell occurred in the Office of the Medical Examiner, Nita City, on July 11, 2013. The body is received from hospital unclad and without accompanying clothing.

External Examination

The body is that of a black male, 34 years old, approximately 5 feet 11 inches, with a weight of 200 pounds. The black scalp hair is short and exhibits a pattern of male baldness. The face is covered by a black full beard and moustache, both having some gray. The oral cavity contains natural teeth and pink, healthy gums. The shoulders, arms, and legs are symmetrical. The belly is relatively flat with a surgical scar across the belly two inches below the navel. Postmortem changes consist of fully developed rigor in both the small and large joints in the body.

Evidence of Therapy

A nasogastric tube extends from the left nostril. A tracheal tube protrudes from the left corner of the mouth. There is a generalized edema, or an abnormal amount of interstitial fluid under the skin, throughout Mr. Powell's entire body. The most interstitial fluid has accumulated around the eyes, lips, and genitalia. A catheter extends out of the right groin. A hospital bracelet with the name "Steven Powell" is on the patient's left wrist.

Evidence of Injury

Virtually the entire body has reddened in appearance. This is most likely due to the significant loss of epidermal pigment in the outer-most layer of skin. The head, face, and left hand have only a few small areas of scalding. There is moderate sparing of the neck, digits of the right hand, scrotum, gluteal crease, and on the soles of the feet.

Cause of death

Multisystem organ failure and shock secondary to massive severe burns.

Thomas Ryan, ME Date: July 11, 2013

Exhibit 6

TOXICOLOGY AND PHARMACOLOGY REPORT

City of Nita

Office of the Medical Examiner

Case Number: 3271-08

Name: Powell, Steven

Age: 34

Race: B

Sex: M

The toxicology analyses were performed in order to detect the presence of the following agents (or classes of agents):

	Analgesics	√	Ethanol (Alcohol)		Quinine
√	Anticonvulsants		Ethchlorvynol	√	Hypnotics/Sedatives
√	Antidepressants		Fentanyl		Solvents
√	Antihistamines		Heavy Metals	√	Stimulants
√	Benzodiazepines		Heroin		THC
	Carbon Monoxide		PCP		
	Cocaine	√	Pseudoephedrine		
	Cyanide		Phenobarbital		

Toxicology and Clinical Pharmacology Findings:

Trace amounts of the above substances were found, but would have not caused any level of impairment as to have played a contributory factor in this accident.

John Samuels   Date: July 18, 2013

John Samuels Toxicologist

Exhibit 7

Giant Paper, Inc.

Employment Log (Day Shift)

Date: July 9, 2013

Employees on Duty (9 a.m. – 5 p.m.):

Supervisors	Laborers	Finishers	Hydrapulper Technicians
Lowell Smith	Mike Mendenhall	Sam Jacobs	Steve Powell
	Paula Robertson	Chris Joseph	Ed Reynolds
	Ken Smyth	Joe Brown	
	Robert Hopvan	Dave Parks	
	Marge Wilson	Phil Dawson	
	Jim Mullen	Kim Staley	
	Andrew Kim	Mike Miller	
	Joe Walker	Carla Coker	
	Mike Brace	Bob Allen	
	Brandon Lee	Brock James	
	Joe Smith	Henry White	
	John Brooks		

Supervisor's Signature: Date: July 9, 2013

Lowell Smith

Lowell Smith

Exhibit 8

Giant Paper, Inc.

Accident Report

Date:	July 9, 2013
Time:	11:15 a.m.
Location:	Beater Room (Hydrapulper Room)
Injured Employee(s):	Steven Powell
Report Prepared By:	Lowell Smith

Description of Events: On July 9, 2013, Steven Powell was the hydrapulper operator of 603 in the beater room. There was only one forklift operator on duty that day. Steve was manually loading paper stock into the hydrapulper. No more stock was supposed to be loaded until the forklift used for 603 was fixed and in operation again. Steven Powell was most likely adding stock to the feed hole using a broom or by hand, and he may have slipped in. A broom was found near the entrance to the feed hole to the hydrapulper. There were no witnesses. No one knows how long he was in there before some coworkers and I got him out of the vat. We had trouble pulling him out because his skin was coming off when we tried to grab him by the arm. When we got him out, he was screaming, "I'm hot! I feel like I'm on fire!" We immediately called 911 and then ripped his shirt off. The EMTs arrived a few minutes after they were called and took Steve Powell to the hospital.

Exhibit 9

Giant Paper, Inc.

Employment Report

Employee: Steven Powell

Hired On: January 17, 2001

Employment Expired On: July 9, 2013

Reason: Work injury resulting in death

Jobs Held at Giant Paper: Laborer, Rewinder, Hydrapulper Technician

Compensation of Jobs Held at Giant Paper:

- Laborer $18/h
- Rewinder $22/h
- Hydrapulper Technician $25/h

Supervisors Evaluation: (Worst 1–10 Best)

- Work Ethic: 8
- Technical Skills: 8
- Mental Disposition: 7
- Physical Disposition: 7
- Health Issues: none
- Violence Issues: none
- Substance Abuse Issues: known to use alcohol regularly, rumored to use cocaine

Exhibit 10

GIANT PAPER, Inc.

REPORT OF CORRECTIVE ACTION

EMPLOYEE NAME: Steven Powell

CLASS: Rewinder

DESCRIBE THE INFRACTION: Intoxicated while at work

DATE OF INFRACTION: February 3, 2010

TYPE OF ACTION:

VERBAL WARNING [ ]

WRITTEN WARNING [ ]

SUSPENSION (5 DAY) [X]

From: February 6, 2010 to February 10, 2010

Exhibit 11

Giant Paper, Inc.

Safety Video Acknowledgement Page

I, Steven Powell, hereby state that I watched the Hydrapulper Safety Video provided by my employer, Giant Paper, Inc., on the 6th day of July, in the year 2013.

I understood the video and it helped me to consider the safety hazards and risks associated with using the hydrapulper machine.

Steven Powell

Steven Powell

Exhibit 12

INTRODUCTION OF HYDRAPULPER SAFETY VIDEO

This safety video is for the SuperPulper hydrapulper model 2000. This safety video is merely illustrative of the correct and safe practices relating to the operation and use of the hydrapulper machine. This introductory list is in no way exhaustive of all the safety concerns that should be understood before anyone uses this machine. Before using any SuperPulper brand hydrapulper, you should watch the entire safety video.

The hydrapulper machine is used to slurry paper pulp. Paper products are dropped into the hydrapulper that contains very hot water. The hydrapulper uses an auger mechanism at the bottom of the machine to churn the water and paper mix. This creates a homogeneous mixture that is essential to the paper making process.

Safety Rules and Concerns:

1. Be aware of your surroundings.
2. Wear your safety glasses at all times.
3. If steam fogs your safety glasses, move away from the hydrapulper before taking off your glasses.
4. Do not use the hydrapulper if you are dizzy.
5. The heat of the pulp and the steam it produces can be disorienting. If at any time you feel fatigued or confused, step away from the hydrapulper.
6. Using the hydrapulper can be dangerous.
7. Do not use the hydrapulper while under the influence of any drugs or alcohol.

Exhibit 13

Hydrapulper Feed Hole

Exhibit 14

Cable in Front of Hydrapulper

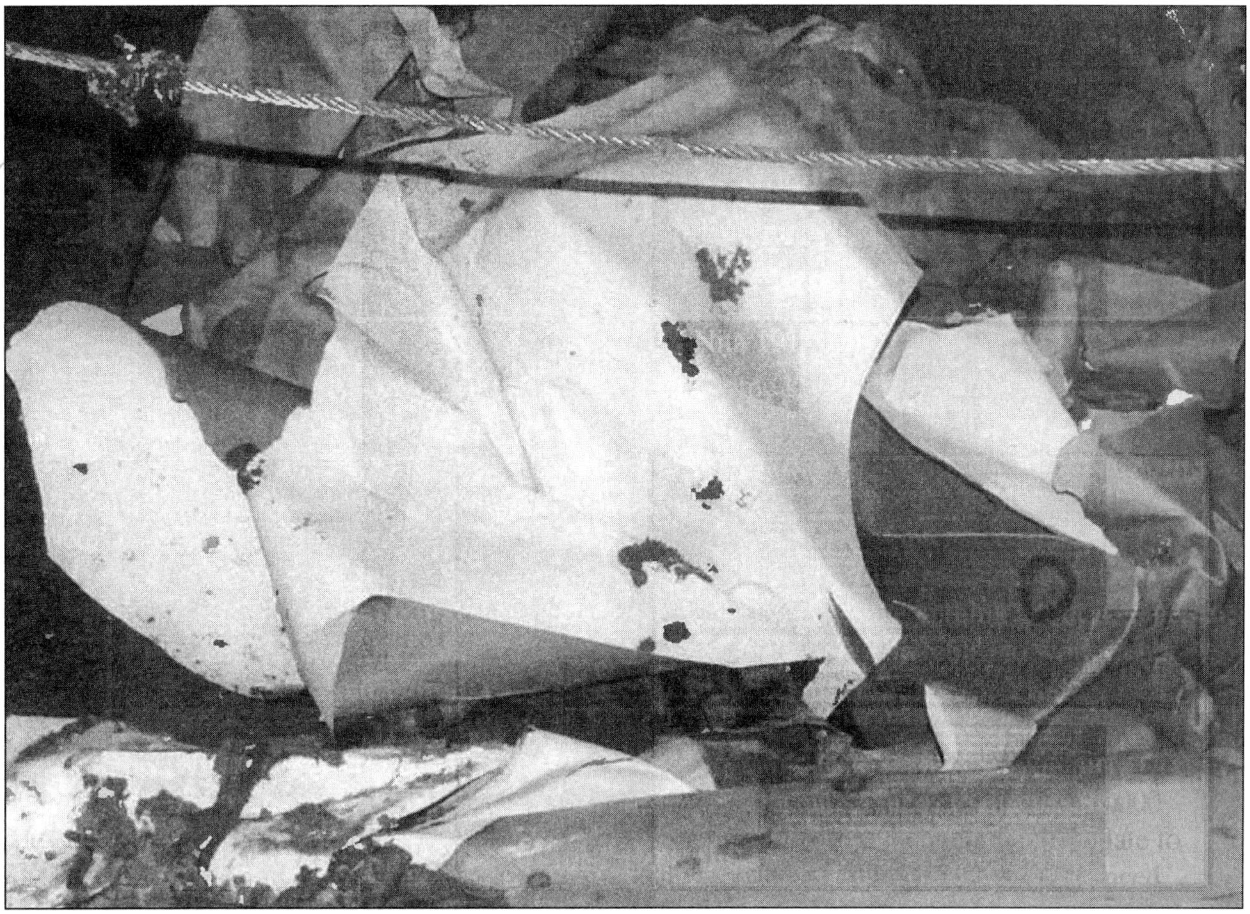

Exhibit 15

Trash in Hydrapulper Room

Exhibit 16

Animation Photo 1

Exhibit 17

Animation Photo 2

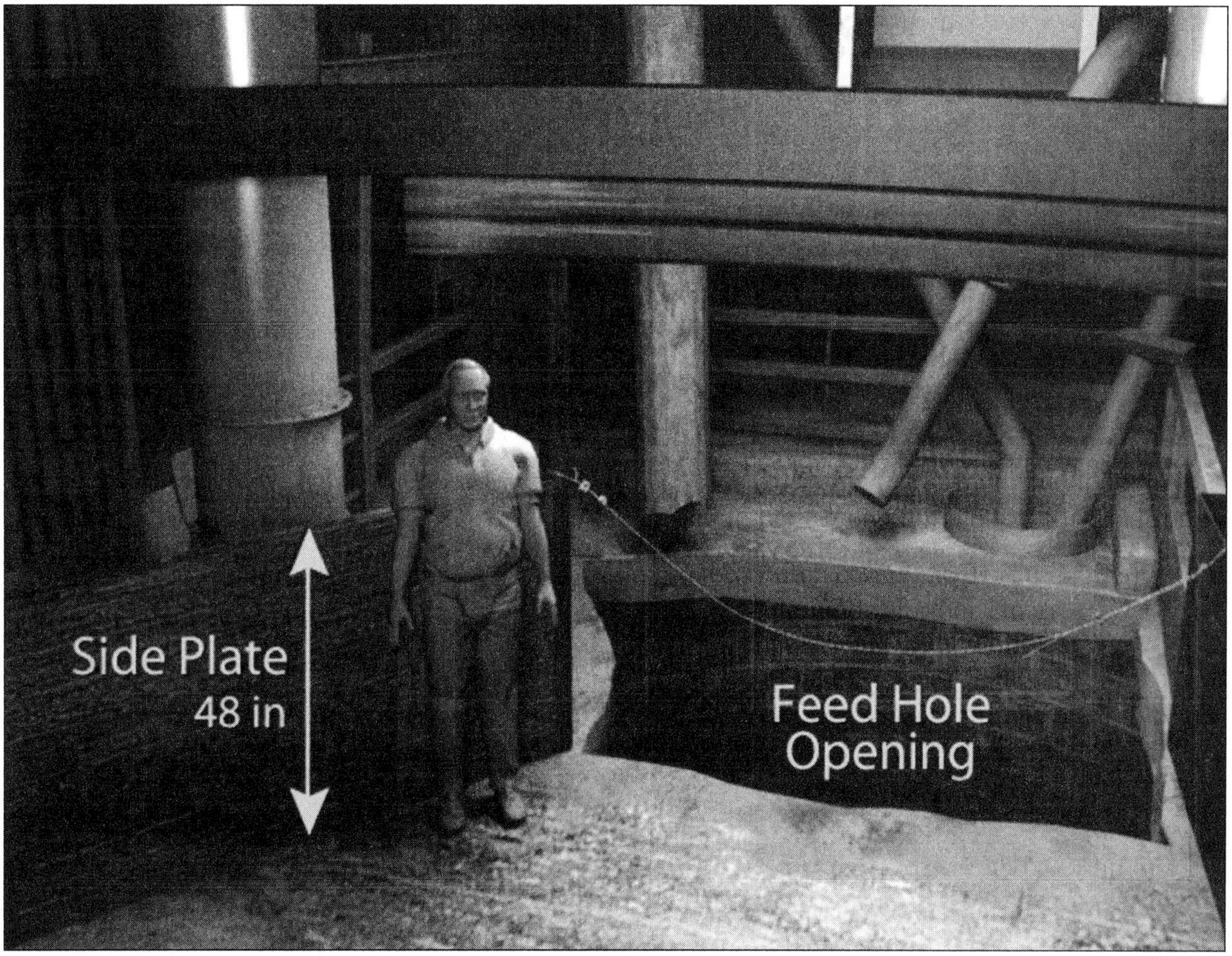

Exhibit 18

Animation Photo 3

Exhibit 19

Animation Photo 4

Exhibit 20

Animation Photo 5

Exhibit 21

Animation Photo 6

Exhibit 22

Animation Photo 7

Exhibit 23

Animation Photo 8

Exhibit 24

Animation Photo 9